Once a farmer and his wife wanted a son. Even one as small as a thumb!

A magician heard them. He cast a spell…and Tom appeared!

Tom was as small as a thumb! So they called him Tom Thumb!

Tom went everywhere.

One day he jumped into a cake!

"Don't eat me!" he said.

Once a bird got Tom and dropped him into the lake.

Tom started to swim...

A big fish ate him! Quickly, Tom's father caught the fish and took it home.

"Oh, Tom, you're fine!" his mother said when she opened the fish. "I was scared!"

One day, Tom was working with the horse. "Go left," he whispered …
"Go right," …
"Stop!"

Two bad men got Tom and the horse.
"You can work for us!" they said.

"Go into this rich man's house and get his money." Tom was scared.

Tom whispered. "Go left,"…
"Right,"… "Stop!"
and took the bad men to the police station!

"What a clever little boy!" said the police officer. "Well done!"

Tom went to see the king and queen.
"Well done, Tom," they said.

Tom quickly went to his house.
"I'm here!" he said.
His mother and father were very happy.

ACTIVITIES

BEFORE YOU READ

**Look at the pictures in the book.
What can you see? Put a ✓ next to the word.**

- ☐ an apple
- ☐ a little boy
- ☐ a fish
- ☐ a burger
- ☐ a cake
- ☐ an orange
- ☐ a magician
- ☐ a butterfly
- ☐ a dog
- ☐ eggs
- ☐ a guitar
- ☐ a knife

AFTER YOU READ

Read the words and then draw and color a picture of Tom Thumb.

Tom Thumb is very small.

He is standing next to a flower.

He is wearing a red coat and green boots.

He is smiling.

The sky is blue.

It is very sunny.

15

Pearson Education Limited
Edinburgh Gate, Harlow
Essex CM20 2JE, England
and Associated Companies throughout the world.

ISBN 978-0-582-42846-1

First published by Librairie du Liban Publishers, 1996
This adaptation first published 2000 under licence by Penguin Books
© 2000 Penguin Books Limited
Illustrations © 1996 Librairie du Liban

9 10 8

Series Editors: Annie Hughes and Melanie Williams
Tom Thumb, Level 2, retold by Marie Crook

Designed by Shireen Nathoo Design
Illustrated by Francesca Duffield

All rights reserved; no part of this publication may be reproduced, stored in a retrieval system, or transmitted in any form or by any means, electronic, mechanical, photocopying, recording, or otherwise, without the prior written permission of the Publishers.

Printed in China
SWTC/08

Published by Pearson Education Limited in association with Penguin Books Ltd,
both companies being subsidiaries of Pearson Plc

For a complete list of titles available in the Penguin Young Readers series please write to your local Pearson Education office or contact: Penguin Readers Marketing Department, Pearson Education, Edinburgh Gate, Harlow, Essex, CM20 2JE.